Carlos Picks a Pet

by Ann Rossi

PEARSON

Scott
Foresman

Editorial Offices: Glenview, Illinois • Parsippany, New Jersey • New York, New York
Sales Offices: Needham, Massachusetts • Duluth, Georgia • Glenview, Illinois
Coppell, Texas • Ontario, California • Mesa, Arizona

ISBN: 0-328-13144-X

16 V010 15 14 13

Carlos was happy. He was on his way to the animal shelter to get a pet!

"A pet is a big responsibility," said his mom.

"Pets have lots of needs," said his dad.

Carlos said, "I can learn about the needs pets have. Then I'll know which one I want!"

Carlos and his parents went to the animal shelter. First, Carlos looked at the rabbits. Some were napping. Others were busy chewing. Carlos learned that rabbits chew a lot. Some of the things they chew can hurt them. Pet rabbits need to stay in cages so they can stay safe.

Carlos thought about having a rabbit. When it is out of its cage, it could sit on his lap. But what if the rabbit chewed something that could hurt it? That would be bad! Maybe a rabbit was not the right pet to pick.

Next, Carlos dashed over to the dogs. The dogs barked and yapped. They wagged their tails. Carlos thought of the fun he would have teaching tricks to a dog. It could fetch and roll over. Then Carlos learned that dogs need to be walked more than one time each day.

Carlos thought about having a dog in the city. He would need to walk the dog every morning. And then he would need to walk it again every afternoon. Maybe a dog was not the right pet to pick.

Last, Carlos saw the cats. He petted a soft black-and-white cat. It would not need to be walked. It would stay safe inside. All it needed was fresh food and water. Cats like to nap and play. They also like to sit on people's laps.

Carlos said, "A cat is just the right pet for me!"

Carlos learned about taking pets to the vet. He promised he would bring his cat to the vet when it was sick.

"I will take it to the vet for checkups too," said Carlos.

So Carlos's parents said he could have a cat. Carlos was so happy.

Back at home, Carlos got out two bowls. He filled one bowl with water. He filled the other bowl with cat food. He put the two bowls in front of his new cat. The cat drank the water. It ate from the bowl. Carlos was taking care of his own pet!

Carlos's first day with his cat was over. The cat still needed a name!

"I will call him Spots, because he is black and white," Carlos said.

The cat purred. Carlos went to sleep with a big smile on his face.

Food for Kittens and Cats

Young cats are called kittens. Kittens stop drinking their mother's milk very early. Once they have stopped, they should be fed four times a day. At three months old they should be fed three times a day. When they turn six months old, they should be fed twice a day. They should be fed twice a day for the rest of their lives.

Week of: __9/1/14__

Monday	Tuesday
Quick Check: Brainstorm animals that would make good pets. What needs would a pet have?	Quick Check: What were the animals that Carlos was choosing between yesterday?
Book: Carlos Picks a Pet Level: H	
Story Introduction Carlos is going to get a pet, what pick should he choose? Stop at p. 9 and Predict which pet Carlos will choose.	Re-read the book: Partner Read Talk about what this should look like and sound like.
Picture Walk Text Feature: Explain the **thought bubble** that is above Carlos' head on the different pages. p.3 finger frame shelter responsibility	Book Discussion: Focus on Comprehension Strategy for this week's stories. Setting and Characters How might the animals in the story have been different, if Carlos were choosing a pet on a farm?
Whisper Read Read to Self while coach listens in as you read.	Journal Writing: What type of pet would be good for you? Write your answer using the words needs and responsibility.
Word Work	Share: Share written responses in the group.
Assignment: Read text at home	No assignment